MOLLY

ILLUSTRATOR: SHYA

MW00852727

I Kissed THE DEVIL

IN THE POURING RAIN

I Kissed the Devil in the Pouring Rain
Copyright © 2021 by Molly Dickin. All rights reserved.

No part of this book may be used or reproduced in any manner whatsoever
without written permission, except in the case of brief quotations embodied in
critical articles and reviews. For more information, e-mail all inquiries to
info@mindstirmedia.com.

Published by Mindstir Media, LLC
45 Lafayette Rd | Suite 181 | North Hampton, NH 03862 | USA
1.800.767.0531 | www.mindstirmedia.com

Printed in the United States of America

ISBN-13: 978-1-7368410-9-9

DEDICATIONS

For my fiancé, Nate, for not only putting up with my working on this book for days on end, but for being my constant support and staying up late to listen to whatever poem I had just written that I absolutely had to read out loud immediately, this book is for you

For every classmate, professor, family member, friend and stranger who entertained me by reading my work and was not afraid to critique the hell out of it so that I may become a better writer, this book is for you

For the people out there, who, like me growing up, always wished to be exposed to more writers who talked bluntly about the realities of coming of age, this book is for you

Lastly, for every muse, magnetizing or devastating, terrifying or beautiful, enthusiastic or discouraging, real or fictional, who gave me something to write about, this book is for you

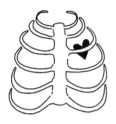

I KISSED THE DEVIL
IN THE POURING RAIN

I.

I kissed the devil in the pouring rain
My hair getting heavier by the second
And his grip on my neck lightened
For a moment and I think I saw God
In the reflection of the puddle I was standing in
Scolding me shamefully, but I didn't care
Those midnight delights were far more tempting
I'd trade a flower for that scripture on your rib
In a heartbeat, no questions asked

Faded floral on basement couches
Consumed me because your Armani
Lingered just a little bit longer than the cedary cigar smoke
Of a nearly forgotten past lover and I dared God
To show his face again in the brown glass bottle
I could see out of the corner of my glazed over eyes
From beneath your leather and cross with the date
Of your friend who was killed on your chest
Before you changed glasses for a diamond earring
And took up brown leaves as a living, just like your daddy

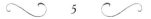

II.

I kissed the devil in the pouring rain
And I prayed for more sinful nights
That snowy powder on your razor had nothing
On that sugar white scar on my knee
Thanks for that souvenir by the way
It tasted sweet as drops of blood I lost
By the mouth of the river
Making love in damp grass there
Sure did a number on that

Blackjack no fear bullshit, you can't lie to me
I heard your heartbeat in the pouring rain
Once before God tried to claim you
And you promised that he wouldn't
Taunting him miserably
Because you weren't that good
No need to point out that I already knew
From the mark on my throat to the tar in your veins
Exactly where you were heading

I kissed the devil goodbye in the pouring rain

PORCELAIN BEAUTY QUEENS

Black limousines and karaoke
Dripping in diamonds
Lips lined with Honey Jack
A halo of smoke coating you
And short party dresses
That would mortify our mothers
With smirking dares
And wicked jokes of Russian roulette
You preying on the
Wild streaks we were
Ordered to kill
But we couldn't seem to shake
The urge to kill ourselves
Slowly
As if we were
Porcelain beauty queens
Who would stay plastic
And liquored up forever
And that was somehow beautiful

DIVE BAR BLUES

Dive bars calling our names
Begging *come dance for us*
Under the dim red lights
Catcalls of men filling voids
Because they'd rather pretend
For a night with others
Than stay home alone looking at faces
In photographs of lovers they lost
And I see you in the corner
Quietly nursing a scotch
Wearing leather and tired eyes
That have seen more
Than most could imagine
And in that brief moment
The cheering blurs away
And my lip turns up
Whispering to you that
I bet my secrets are darker
And I long to sit with you
In the silence of our tragedies
Letting ourselves indulge
In a rollercoaster of sins
We swore we'd never speak of

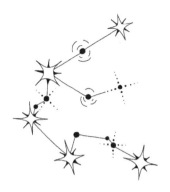

HELL-BENT

3 a.m. whispers of sapphire secrets
From your eyes dancing with the devil
In a way that would scar your mother for life
And dreamlands of the gates of heaven
Which we pray we only gaze at
Until we are inevitably greeted with God's presence
An untimely joke preying on your
Sheer lack of vulnerability
Rooftop cigarettes, the ashes our stars
As you map out constellations on my rib
And dare me to risk everything
For a soul hell-bent on loving me only slightly less
Than he hates himself

QUIET

You touched me too roughly
An unwavering distance in your eyes
For me to think we would last
I told you when you first kissed me
That I knew you would break my heart
I only asked that you gave me
Enough memories to reminisce on
During days like these
When the ocean is quiet
And my mind is quiet
And the whole damn world
Feels calm and turns perfectly
Because on days like these
I tend to crave absolute chaos
Like the cherry red fingerprints
That you gifted me with
As you gripped my hips
And blanketed my body with yours
In your Mustang under Miami skies
The smell of a freshly lit blunt
Between your calloused fingers
After a long day on the job
Getting high and getting into another fight
Because fuck your dad's advice to walk away
From another drunk challenging your manhood
He ended up in prison anyways
A one-way ticket and still your sister wasn't safe
You know, sometimes I still think about
That night at Ricky's house
Where we danced on his mother's oak table
And you said you loved me

Before passing out onto a chair
Turning it into kindling
Because you took too much
And how I should have been embarrassed
By the state of you
Slurring your threats at the guys
Who were videotaping
Blood on your head, another scar for me to clean
But all I could think about
Was that in that moment
You were mine and you loved me
And anyone who saw the footage
Would have proof of how lucky I was
To be the girl that belonged to
The equally fucked up and gorgeous man on the ground
You used to show up at three in the morning
Reeking of whiskey and cheap cigarettes
And I never cared where you'd been
Only that when you started to sober up
You came to me
And I loved that you needed me too
Bloodshot eyes looking into mine
Telling stories about how one day
We would run away together
Pocket a box of hair-dye
Jump the turnstiles and head somewhere new
I think it was just me who knew
That it would never happen
You'd fall out of love or get caught a final time
No more chances and you'd get
Locked up like your dad
And I'm grateful forever
For all of the highs you gave me
Years later and my heart races quickly

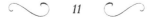

With the most thrilling guilt
As I relive our fighting and our fucking
Our lying and our loving
Telling my stories in ink
To keep you alive a little bit longer

SANGRIA

Spanish music moving your poetry
Tasting guitar chords on your tongue
Like brilliant tangerines
Juicy and ripe, summer in love
Closing wooden doors as we dance
Cast-iron cooking infuses our noses
Spices and sangria line my lips
As you make my stories into art
With the sculpture of your body

TWO WORLDS COLLIDING

We come to life, clinging to endless summer nights
Whispering secrets as we dance among constellations
Trading beautiful promises, our golden era
That no soul, no matter how hungry for war, could take from us
We felt like Gods, dancing too electrically to die quite yet
Outlasting a fate we were told was decided a lifetime ago
Defying time apart and an almost forgotten past together
For two worlds colliding in spectacular slow motion
Our longing put to rest for what I only hope will be forever and then some
As we live the way we finally realized we were created for

ON ARTISTS AND DYING YOUNG

I thought I was born to shine
Brightly and explode
Too soon, dying young
Leaving behind a glorious
Legacy of secrets
That could fill a library of books
Wild glimpses of lasting advice
Over a blunt you'd never forget the taste of
After a night of dancing on tables
In shimmering spotlights
Lacy bras on floors
Behind closed doors
With a promise that I'd
Never get attached
Lipstick prints on your mind
For a boy who could
Never turn me good
Now I write behind a pair
Of tired glasses
My cup filled with coffee
And my nights
Filled with dreamless slumber

MISTRESS

Sadness sold me on powder
And parties only slightly quieter
Than the voices in my head
Which I threaten to silence with pills
And lovers estranged from faces and names
And glamorous nightclubs with golden flasks
But they call my bluff
For they know that I'll come crawling back for more
For my sadness is my mistress
And I have never loved harder

WORSHIP

I took your weight between the curves of my hips
And I prayed
I didn't have a God that I worshipped
Let me worship you
I hope you know that's what my lips were saying
Tucked behind a red plastic cup for safe keeping
Your eyes wide, cheeks flushed
In the bedroom upstairs at the party
I think it was October or maybe September on the island
Time used to make sense
Back when you were mine forever
But now I'm alone
In the dark I make my own galaxies
That hang above me, no longer unafraid
Pieces of you-shaped-reminders

About being so lost in someone
That I begin to find myself
Dance above me as my only company

TAFFY

You had a beautifully dangerous mind

Graying hair and years of unspoken poetry
Stuck between your teeth like taffy
Velvet secrets after midnight
That I burdened you with, my darling
Knowing you were already lost in me
Promises traced back to the first time
I reached across that desk
Pleading for your adoration
A reckless request on my lips
I never dreamed you would entertain

CALIFORNIA

Hearing your voice over static
Three time zones away
Felt more guilt-ridden

Than sitting by your side
Your hand fidgeting
Half a ruler's length
Away from my thigh
Before I knew of your craving
To hold me like you owned me
Something sacred
That only the devil could witness
Making me long tragically
For something I never
Thought that I needed

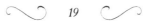

AN ODE TO MY HOMETOWN

For I swore she would be the death of me one day
Seventeen looking like a lifetime ago
In photographs with friends who were mine forever
Until we were no longer lonely enough to need each other
Cherry rosé and goodbyes where I'd hold her close
Devastation heavy in my heart when I knew it was the last time
She waved me off fondly and I looked back with longing
Her dark skies above pine trees had her in my prayers
Night after night until I forgot what it was like to be loved by her
The feeling of her crisp air on empty streets
When it finally got dark enough after midnight for me to call her my own
Memories stopped being painful to reminisce on
So she faded from my thoughts and into the death
Of a girl I knew I didn't love anymore
A girl I couldn't love anymore

ORANGE SODA

Orange soda used to line
The crease on the corner
Of your lip that now
Tastes like 90 proof
With a hint of lime
And it stings my Jungle Red
As I stare vacantly
Out the bay window
At the graying fog
Dusting the city skyline
And I search for a faint pulse
Blood pumping
From a lone heart

SLOW DANCING
WITH ELLA FITZGERALD

Red dresses and rivieras
Moonlight dancing
On beautiful patios
With stones created by God
For lifting us up to the heavens
Under lights wrapping around pergolas
And whispers of promises in naive ears
For souls who love
Timelessly for eternities
That last as long as
One side of my jazz record

EIGHTEEN

You were exactly the kind of man
That I was continuously seeking out
Eighteen and I was lonely and insatiable
Searching for a newfound freedom
In empty wine bottles
And ripped fishnets on your kitchen island
Your eyes testing me to see
If I was as much of a maniac as I promised I was
You tasted dangerous
Not the kind at fifteen when you sneak out
To meet a boy from school under a streetlight down the block
Or the kind when you find yourself
Scanning the room for an exit plan
Because an evil came over him
As you witnessed him turn into his dad before your eyes
To both of your horror
But the kind when your arms lifted me up
And you loved me like a woman
A woman who wasn't fragile or naive
But a woman who felt nothing but ecstasy
As I dug my nails into your inked back
And watched your eyes turn
From smirk to satisfaction under moonlight

FATAL EUPHORIA

Dreamily lit balconies
My nickname on your lips
Tattoos and manhattans
Sipping on bad decisions
That you're about to make
With a woman that will
Never compare to that
Fatal euphoria we created

LONELY DREAMERS

We were lonely dreamers
Lawless without a place
To call our own
Your words the grounding
Of castles filled with a hope
I grew out of when I was
Young and serenading my city
Love affairs with art
That were bound to be
The death of me one day
Until one day turned into
A lifetime of isolation
Free from degradation
Why couldn't I be happy
Why couldn't I love her enough
Why couldn't she hurt me
Metal swords slicing
Through her convictions
Her lights through my window
Once tempted me
To roam the streets
In search of something
To make me feel alive
Am I too far gone from her
Yet taking up undeserved space
To ask her to love me again
For her to hold
My weary head
In the back of a taxi
Filled with cheap perfume
And cigarette smoke

For her to give my body
Rhythm under lights
Of lime and peaches
For her to hold me
And sing to me Sinatra
As I'm falling asleep
Trying to make out constellations
Through polluted air
For her forgiveness
And my selfish audacity
To ask her to try a little harder
To keep me next time

INTANGIBLE

I fall in love with people
Who will destroy me
Because when I am hurt
I become beautiful
An intangible soul
Whose eyes hold dark secrets
That you can't understand
Broken and charming
An enigma you want to marvel at
Some kind of morbid fascination
Or maybe you want to save me
But my darling
I am too shattered to care
For your good-natured manner

FIRECRACKER

You were born
To live among
The stars
You set fires
That blaze in
My warming soul
A life too peaceful
To feel alive
Awaken me
If your fire
Is hell
I will gladly
Dance for eternity
With the devil
Singe my fingertips
I'll trace your lies
Down your back
And cast them
Into the sky
A slave for
Your flames

BAR AT THE BELLAGIO

Paying for my crimes
With only an empty glass
And a little white powder
As my company
I'm sick and I'm certain
That you'd beg for me
If only you knew
How depraved I am
Have a drink
Let's not talk
About the lifetime
Of secrets we share
Let's breathe them in
And begin to forget them
In the bed upstairs
I'll slip a Benjamin
To the bartender
For sealed lips
Another Bellagio secret
If you promise to leave
In the morning
Tomorrow I'll drink
Alone again
Feeding my paper
With guilt over you
Sins in the ink
Giving me just enough
Exhilaration
Until I need someone
To forget with again

INDULGENCE

Spending my nights cruising around
In fast cars with girls with loose rules
Drying my tired eyes
Feeling infinite for an evening
And in those irreplaceable moments
That's all I care about
Drawing me into your car
Shadowy figures as a backdrop
To our love affair
That I would never indulge in
If we weren't frowned upon

UNDER THE LIGHTS

Dirty secrets under the static
Of bleacher speakers
At the Friday night football game
Spotlight on player 52 in a long line
Who word vomit victories
Without worry of conquests being questioned
As Corona clad hands beckon
Me to answer to their glassy eyes
If what you told them is true
About our basement couch christening
That at sixteen decided the fate
Of further shared bedroom door whispers
And accusations far more evil
Than your hands in my hair
And the smoke on your motorcycle jacket
That you wrapped me in
After swigging 40s
By the fence in the woods
Where you convinced me that a zipper
Was more than something leading
To a button on faded denim

CRUMBLING KINGDOMS

Fallen angels and cigar smoke
On terraces as they laugh
About crumbling kingdoms
Drowning in top-shelf liquor
Never turning down a dare
Because we grasp for unholiness
When our loneliness begins
To feel a little too honest

BUTTERFLIES

Scattered paper trails
Through your back garden
Where I was your lover
For a moment in time
When butterflies were
No sacred scarcity
And we laughed about
You breaking my heart
Before I fell hard enough
For that possibility
To feel the slightest
Bit tangible

MY SIN, MY SOUL

You held the power of Nabokov in your arms
And I lived for the littlest moments
That meant everything to me back then
Tired hands sculpting a beautifully poisonous world
For a girl who was desperate for everything
That I had been sheltered from
It made no sense for me to understand
The darkness and desire of a man
I never should have loved, but couldn't stop
Soft pink filters, swinging in slow motion
Your hand on my leg as we'd drive
In your red convertible, laughing until we were dizzy
You told me one afternoon at your desk
That I made you feel decades younger
And I wondered why you'd want
To feel out of control like I did, unable to live for myself
I envied your aged perspective, my curiosity piquing
At the power and money you had
Degrees and awards lining the wall behind us
Rusting dreams covered in golden lust
For you, my darling, as you cradled my head
And we danced a little too slowly
To rock music from long before my time

TATTOOS

Dream of me darling
In euphoric delight
Of the way we traded
War stories and
I traced your tattoos
Which I wondered about
But never asked the meaning
Because I knew
How tortured you were
And the shame of your darkness
Lured me in majestically
Forfeiting any better judgement
I may have had

CONTROL

Your teeth sink deep into my neck
With such a demanding conviction
That I feel like I belong to you already
Like the strength in your wrists
Could tell me where I'll end up tonight
On the plumb corduroy of your best friend's couch
Or on the gray leather in the back of your Volvo
While the clasp of your hand
Begged for my continued silence
So long as you got what you needed
Until the curve of my collarbone melded with your lips
For a moment, the zipper on your leather pants
Was the only thing I knew was real
And I searched your eyes for an understanding
That no part of me is here
Looking for a sanity that does not exist
And I'd be devastated to find out
That it did

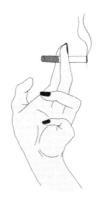

ḢAUNTED PARADISE

Whiskey and hand-rolled cigarettes
Forgotten secrets come to life
Glistening in your eyes like
A haunted paradise
Begging me not to ask the questions
That burn in my throat
Matchsticks and playing cards
Across a dimly lit table
And I can already tell
That you're too burned out
To come alive again
In the way that my
Smirk is begging you to

MATH CLASS

I liked the rule breakers
Age thirteen and I could tell you without hesitation
All the ways in which
The boy in class who sat next to me had me in a daze
My stubborn mind melting like butter
I would shudder with the delicious taste of guilt
Not because he called me pretty, which he did
But because of the danger that lurked behind
Each one of his words, no longer a kid
My eyes danced
Back before makeup and breakups
That left them all puffy
Tears down my face, my nose feeling stuffy
He was smooth, not awkward or nervous
Already knew how he liked to be serviced
I hated boring, I hated polite
I wanted a boy unafraid to bite
I was always getting in trouble
Sneaking out to make friends with the devil
The cute boy from math class was the first on my level
My parents worried that he corrupted me
You see, I was anything but what a girl should be
I'd been searching forever
For something that dirty
Unsturdy he ignited me, delighted me
Invited me to be a version of myself
That I always had to hide
So I invited him inside

GHOST

Tracing a ghost
Made out of ink
You were in love
With being haunted
The fear, the loss
Once they became
Familiar to you
Breathing without them
Was something you
Couldn't go back to
I understood that
Better than anybody
Begging my demons
To show their faces
And your hands
Poured secrets
Into my body
That neither of us
Could say out loud
With each kiss
Your darkness
Became mine too
And we brought to life
A brand new tragedy

TRAGICALLY

I loved you tragically
Beautifully, tragically
Irrational days
And uninhibited nights
Between the sheets
Unthinkable acts
Wrapped in silk
Further down the rabbit hole
We were spinning
Tangled in our fears
Until they no longer existed
Relinquishing our rules
Dignity sparse

WOUNDS

When I drink a glass too many
Of my favorite scotch
My words and thoughts
Tend to muddle together
Murky water realizations
That there's something
Evil in my veins
Something of yours
That you left behind
That I'm holding onto aggressively
Keeping your wounds
Safely guarded
In case you return for them

MADLY

I loved you
A little too madly
To allow myself
To save you
From me

PASTEL MOONLIGHT

I miss claiming that I hated the way
That I would hear you talk about me
Torturing me with glimpses of our
Bonfire nights and driving to
The middle of absolutely nowhere
Under deep navy skies
Because we were young and sleepless
With our dreams during daylight
And with darkness came
Vivid sensuality of forest dreamscapes
In truth I loved hearing my name
Roll off your tongue

When you'd mention your body on mine
And the way I'd lust after you
Keeping private my hand on rough denim
With yours on the wheel
And the way you twirled me into you
Holding me so closely

That your pulse was made rhythmic drumbeat
To the words you whispered under pine trees
Piece by piece giving yourself to me
As you would invite me
Deeper into your world
Under the sanctity of pastel moonlight

HIDEAWAYS

Lemon trees and golden rays
Hazy hideaways where time
Ceases to exist
And for a beautiful moment
I'm in love without feeling you
Slipping from my hands
And into a memory
Because I have a special knack
For making a mess
Out of beautiful things

PHOTOPHOBIA

I painted you in the dark
As a villain lurking in the shadows
Or in the woods lying in wait
To rip the innocence off my body
And discard it on the floor
Tangled with your belt buckle
Behind locked doors
Because I couldn't admit
That your shadow didn't cover my light
It illuminated my dark

BURDENS

He was perfectly enigmatic
Leaving a trail of pretty girls
Pining after him in his wake
Never staying for long enough
To collect a phone number
A weary traveler
He carried burdens like
Loose change making music
In the bottom of my purse
And he couldn't love me
But he loved my city
And I loved the lights
Reflecting in his eyes

CABERNET

Something about writing alone
At night with a bottle of cabernet
Has me nostalgic
For the things about you
That I swore disgusted me

FIFTEEN

I fell in love
In the back of your pickup
Under a red plaid blanket
Just before I was asked
To trade the cross on my necklace
For a sweaty football jersey
And four empties
Of mint lime mojito
For eleven minutes of fame
How callous of me to entertain the idea
That your belt buckle
Just might be more enticing
At fifteen than the promise of God
In an empty church basement
Collecting dust from non-believers
That my family warned me about
You would be their nightmare
And soon became mine too
And the ecstasy from that
Was more of a delicious temptation
Than the crystals
Hidden in the wooden trick box
From your dad
On your eighteenth birthday

WATERFALLS

I loved you like
You were replaceable
Screaming matches
And waterfalls
On my cheeks
After midnight
Until we grew
Older and tired
Of making love
Like strangers
Because I couldn't
Let you in
Breaking you repeatedly
Until you couldn't
Take it anymore
And left me
Searching through my past
For something tangible
To prove to myself
That at one time
I was loved by you

ENIGMA

He lived like he'd never known fear
My Gatsby on a spiral staircase
But I knew that he was terrified
He didn't much show affection
Or love anybody to his fullest
But the way that my baby would dance
And laugh at 2 a.m.
Was my oxygen for a time
A time I'll never forget
But only on occasion revisit
To have something so magnetic
So utterly intangible
Between my arms
In a world that needs more magic in it
Was the most electrifying
And soothing sensation
I could possibly imagine

UNRELENTING HEARTBREAK

There was a time
When I thought I would never
Be relieved from the pain
Of loving you
Unrelenting heartbreak
That I kept going back to
Until we kissed goodbye
Not knowing it
Would be the last time
Years between us now
With new memories
You made without me
And a realization
That I've been trying
To torture myself
With old wounds
And depleted attempts
To rip them open
Because I'm craving
A kind of pain
That has been missing
Since you stopped
Loving me

RED LICORICE LINES

Walking down that hallway
Hearing you laugh for the first time in months
And my stomach slides right through the rest of my body
Because I realize your smirk gets slightly bigger
When my pump hits the floor just a little too loudly
I try to turn around but my shaking legs
Can't stop walking in your direction
The closer my heartbeat is to yours
The less nervous I have to be
That you're going to sneak up on me
The things I did to her
You're staring at me now
Wicked brown eyes apologizing in a way
That contradicts the bragging in your voice
The best I ever had
God, the other girls would kill to have you say that about them
But they didn't know you like I did
The 1 a.m. you when your fingers gripped me too tightly in the woods
The you behind the white paint chipped door
Labeled 603 with lies wrapped in satin
And the you that I wore under my sundress
In red licorice lines
I'm going to hit that again

READ LOLITA

Your eyes glistened up at me
As I rolled my stockings
Down my legs, sitting on your counter
Picking up your glass of scotch
My brows raised in a dare
To stop me from breaking the rules
I took a swig, trying desperately
To conceal that this wasn't
Something I usually got up to
It lined my cherry red lips
And I ran my hands
Through your graying hair
Every part of my body pulsing
Because there was so much more
Behind these moments
Than we could ever speak of
Even saying it out loud
Crossed the line in a way
We couldn't turn back from
Read Lolita, you told me
And I fell in love for the first time
I still keep your copy
In the drawer of my nightstand

RESTLESS CRAVINGS

Lips parting legs
Under navy skies
Hungry eyes
Unbreaking promises
We forgot to keep
When we were younger
And burning out
On cheap cigarettes
And one-night stands
That made us
Feel infinite
For a moment
At seventeen
There's an eagerness
In your hands
And years of
Restless cravings
Between us
Desires no one else
Could come close
To filling

GEARS

The faded leather on your body
As I gripped your back
Felt coarse as you ate
My breath away with your teeth
Wrapped in your obsession so tightly
That the tree on my hip comes to life
Like it's waving in the wind
As my body writhes beneath your command
My lips trembling because I fear
You, my dear, when our bodies separate
Until there is a wall of ice
Dividing your reckless
No care in the damn world attitude
From the warm skin
That blankets my tensing bones
That grind together
Like gears unsure how to turn without oil

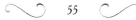

SMALL

You weren't quite honest with me
When you said you wanted to help me
For me to heal between your arms
That would hold me
When I needed somewhere safe to cry
You played me as a damaged fool
And I realized far too late
That you loved me broken
And you wouldn't have had me
Any other way
Your words gave me no strength
As you broke me down only to
Build me up just the tiniest bit
That felt like everything to a girl
Who longed for a place to call home
Finding it between the buttons
Of wrinkled denim shirts
Destroying me a little bit with each kiss
You wanted me weak
And I learned the long and tiring way
That you never felt stronger
Than when I felt small

JEALOUSY

Red glossed lips
And depraved daydreams
Where I forbid myself from
Indulging in a guessing game
Of what you're up to
Or who you're up to
Longing to be the person
Who accuses you of hurting them
I wear jealousy better
Than your other lovers
And my purple teddy
And your empty bottle
Can prove it

ENCHANTING SHADOW

I started loving you
Under pastel moonlight
Secrets turning to
Whispered promises
Your figure outlined
An enchanting shadow
And fingers that
Slip between mine
Like a star being
Wished upon for the first time

FADED

Whispers of daring promises
Made under the bleachers
By a man known for being
Bad news with a constant
High in his eyes that feels
Beautiful for a girl who can't
Help falling in love
With a tragic story

FEVER

Five years later and my stomach
Flips more than I thought was possible
When I stumble across your photograph
Electricity twists and turns throughout my body
As I poorly attempt to convince myself
That it's from the small cup of coffee I sipped on
While popping another record
On the player an hour earlier
There's something different about you
But I can't quite decipher what it is
You still have those earrings you showed up to senior year with
When all the other girls swarmed around you
Bad news upperclassman
Who traded his football jersey and college applications
For a leather jacket and a blunt that never ceased to burn
The writing on your rib is still there
But looks different in a mirrored selfie
Than it did while you were on top of me
On that basement couch
And told me what the ink stood for
You still have that same cocky attitude
That I thought was so ugly on the other guys
But you seemed to wear it so well
That my skin feels ten degrees warmer
When I feel your eyes smirking at me
From underneath your baseball cap
Daring me to resist your tattooed arms
That once propped me up
On your kitchen island and left my blouse
A pile of tattered silk on that tile floor

MARMALADE

You were marmalade lips
A grin on your face as sunlight faded
Cigarette in hand, you would hold me
Promises that I knew were just wishful thinking
But I didn't tell you that
Because I knew you meant them
And there was nothing more beautiful to me
Than watching you dream

YOU WEREN'T LONG FOR THIS WORLD

You told me shortly before you left
That I shouldn't have fallen in love with you
Because you weren't long for this world
Your soul aching day by day
You weren't excited by
The hustle and bustle
Of the city who had been your first lover
Before you cast her aside
Until returning home a tired traveler
And needed somewhere familiar to rest your head
You didn't crave the danger
That came with nights on motorcycles with the guys
Or lust after an impending tranquility
We once prayed we'd feel
When we grew up and grew out of that fast-paced living
Maybe poolside under caramel sunshine or
In a cafe in a small town we could pretend we had always called home
Where we could sleep and watch old movies
And forget that they weren't our stories
Until our own came to an end
Not one that felt too sudden or filled with panic and begging for a solution
But one that felt like an easy farewell
Resting for good in the first place we didn't long to run from

WAVES

He was my waves and I his sand
At the top of the beach
Only reachable at high tide
If his storm was strong enough
To encapsulate me

A TAXI AWAY

I heard your name tonight
For the first time in years
And just like that
I'm sixteen again
Dazzled by fast cars
And men with money
Claiming I gave them life
Party dress on and cigar in hand
Like I knew how to smoke it
Laughter and a whisper
Tucked behind your ear
As you cradled my face
Under polluted skies
And made me feel like
I was born to be the girl
That you'd been dreaming about
Vacant eyes to others
But you knew the longing they held
Reserved for you
At a dinner for two
Your coat draped over my bare shoulders
When that gray king size satin
Was only a taxi away

MY FINGERS BLEED PROMISES

Dancing together
My eyes lingered
A little longer
Than usual
On her collarbone
My lips trace songs
On her neck and
My fingers bleed
Promises into her hips
That I'll probably
Never keep
But all that matters
Is the gin on her breath
And the high
That fills her wild eyes
Her nose is bloody
And her hands fidget
With a crumpled twenty
Our minds racing
Faster than ever before
And the only thing
That I know is real
Is my craving
To make love
To every inch of her

STARRY EYED DAY DREAMERS

With secrets in our hips
And poems on our lips
We torture ourselves indefinitely
With truths that give us
That beautiful kind of pain
An insatiable nostalgia
For the moments when
Longing followed leaving
And being desirable
Meant someone having an affinity
For the untouchable parts of ourselves
That we'd never admit
We're too scared to search for

LIKE RAIN ON COBBLED STREETS

Tears drop onto your lips
Like rain on cobbled streets
Outside cafe windows
Candlelight can't soothe
The war waging
In a beautiful mind
Too delicate for the
World you're living in with me
Tissues and cardigans
Apologies and I'm helpless
At stopping all of your hurt
But I'm trying not to show you
How much it's killing me
The last thing I want is to
Burden you with another worry
Tucking your hair behind your ear
Pretending that loving you
Isn't destroying me

UNDER THE OVERPASS

Secrets wrapped in smoke
Under the overpass
Climbed up your
Leather clad legs
Like a vine up to my tongue
A hint of bourbon
Lingered as the only
Barrier between your
Bare chest and my black lace
Your brown eyes twinkled
With a hint of forever
Divided only by the green grass promise
Of your next fix

SINISTER

There was something sinister
The last time you kissed me
Cinnamon and cigars
Collared sleeves rolled
Lip turned up like you were
Getting revenge for something
I'd chosen to forget years ago
Your eyes betraying your intentions
As we both pretend
That you don't still love me

ALL OVER AGAIN

I'd never been a girl
Who was reeled in
By money and fancy suits
Sleek cars and custom watches
But that afternoon
Unbuttoning your collared shirt
Revealed the same
Ink on your chest
That I traced at sixteen
When you wore
Nothing but denim
And burgundy bruises
After getting in another fight
Wicked in your hands
And a dare in your eyes
Your tie drops to the floor
And I love you like I'm young
And you're dangerous
All over again

I LOVE TO MISS YOU

You're more beautiful to me in golden retrospect
An insatiable force that I love to miss
More than I love being with
Because I'm not free when I'm safe
And I was created to lust after chaos
Just as you were designed to be
Admired by all and understood by so few

SOPHIA

Your red lips stain my cheek
From late night rendezvous
Where the scent of your shampoo
Lingered in my hair
As I lay underneath my white plush comforter
Trying to sleep
But unable to leave the curve of your back
Out of my mind for even a moment
Which may be for the best
As I'd be dreaming of a vortex so deep and so pure
That it could swallow my sins whole
With no further need for repenting
And for just one moment
I wouldn't be too damaged to be seen
By such an evergreen sense of lust
As more than a phone call at 2 a.m.
When you're sick and tired of being clean
And craving the dirty taste of danger
Before sunrise summons you back
And you're at the beck and call of a life
That you're too much of a coward to throw away
For a girl who would give up everything
To pay the check at a dinner for two

HOLLOW

There was something hollow
In the way she kissed me
That very last time
As my hands traced
Once familiar promises
From her lips to her thighs
Aching with a growing unfamiliarity
Knowing full well that she wasn't
Agonizing over our impending goodbye

FAIRY LIGHTS

Being back under these fairy lights
Takes me right to you and I can even
Smell your cologne
You're a fucked up collage with jagged memories

It's the blunt that you rolled and suggested
We get high in the woods and hearing myself agree
Despite my better judgement
It's the taste of your darkest secret on my tongue
The spearmint whispering every reason that
I should run and the ink on your arm
That makes me cave in an instant
It's the amusement that dances on your water lines
When you learn for the first time
Just how much innocence I have left
You could pack it into a Tic Tac container
And still have breathing room

PALMS

Palms lining your face
And I catch a glimpse
Of your infinite hesitation
A pearl ring that she wore
Haunting you in every
Steaming mug of coffee
And click of a TV remote
Aging you years after
Her beauty was suspended
For the rest of time and I want
More than anything
To dream with you
For days on end melting
Into sleepless nights
Discovering constellations
And tracing prayers
On each other's backs
But the palms are
Whispering to me that
Your soul is hers
And how can I compare
To the frozen face
In a sepia photograph
Dancing with laugh lines
Of memories that will
Never be mine

HYMN OF TERRORS

Laying on the small, cold mattress on the floor, tossing and turning
I stare at the discolored taupe walls
Wondering how many people have come before me
Wondering why
Each scratch in the wall, each dent in the floorboard
Another person haunted
By the building or their minds
Maybe both
I dive further under the covers
But nothing drowns out the whispers coming from the hallway
Hearing nightmares carried out
Tales of demons creeping up on one person after another
Choking them from the inside of a bottle
Bleeding them out from the edge of a blade
Penetrating them through the intrusion of an unwanted body
Shrieks, sniffles and the rattling sound of pill bottles opening and closing
Sing eerily into my room
Through the slight crack in the door
A hymn of suffering and history too dark to put into words
Eventually laying me to rest in a low hush

TYPEWRITER

Navy skies darkening
The beat of my heart
Pulsing to the rhythm
Of my typewriter
And the ash from your
Cigar cleanses the sins
I begged your tattooed arms for
A guilty pleasure
Dressed in faded leather

A SIX PACK TOO MANY

It doesn't make any sense
For me to love you still
You've given me every reason
To run and never look back
You've made every inch of me
Tremble with fear
My friends still shudder
When I say your name
Because they can't count
On all their fingers and toes
The ways that you hurt me
But what they didn't see
Was the fire in my body
In your bed when you
Locked the door and
Showed me all your demons
Or the times I rinsed your blood
Off my hands again
Because he took another shot at you
After drinking a six pack too many

DAZZLED

I was intrigued by you
From the first night
You traced your hand on my hip
Before walking outside
And lighting up a joint
Alone on the back porch
Golden embers in your eyes
As you looked me up and down
Solidifying the moment
I became yours
Burgundy fingerprints
Blossomed on my shoulders
Come springtime
That I thanked Ostara for
You were wild and dangerous
Coming alive with
The love you had for haunting me
The most delicious combination
For a girl who was
Dazzled by everything
That could destroy me

FANTASIZING OF A WORLD INSIDE MY HEAD

Your hands, firm but somehow still
Passive, in a way that omits love
Through aggression but gives me
No dark spark to fantasize about
In brief moments of closure
Grasp the horizon of my back
Twirling me into your lies
As we dance a duet of
Cat and mouse that is reflected
In the emerald eyes of a stranger
Who I loved once in a past life
Of bourbon and black lace
And I wonder if his pulse
Still feels the same as it did under
That faded leather after we snuck
Into the playground for a night
Far darker and more thrilling than
You could dream to give me
And tragically don't mind
My fantasizing of a world in my head
That would be tainted
Should you ever take the slightest peek

COLLATERAL

It was my mind that you feared the most
You couldn't fathom my undying need to lose control
A blessing, a temptation
Alluring, but too dangerous to entertain
My words echoed in your head
Long after I slept
My thoughts drawn into a world of terror and insanity
While my body lay still
And you battled yourself in the absence of my voice

WORLD

It is a strange type of loneliness
To have you back in my life
When you're no longer my world

MY BURDEN

Lifetimes I've wasted
Wishing on stars to be understood
By someone as lonely and hurt as I am
For eyes that hold secrets
That I'm afraid to ask about
Like everybody feels
When they look into mine
And it gives me great pain
To acknowledge with full admittance
That this sadness
Is my burden and my soulmate
Intertwined until the end

SARA

There was something about
The way that she twirled
In her plaid skirt
That drove me completely insane
She ignited my veins
As we lay with our backs
Pressed against the floor
And talked about a future
We knew we'd never have
Watching her put on makeup
As watermelon flavored gloss
Dripped down her lips
Forced my knees to
Fight the urge to buckle
She unzipped my dress
And I could feel her hot breath
On my neck as she mouthed
A secret I couldn't hear
And still torture myself
With guesses

VOLATILE

I haven't felt that kind of love since you left
The type that makes me ask myself
If today is the day that our moments become memories
And I wish that I could say that I've grown out of
Longing for something so volatile

RARE WOMAN

She was a truly rare woman
Emerald eyes a masterpiece
Voice like a late-night radio personality
Serenading lonely men with songs
Who are searching for a perfect honey
And the way she rolled cigarettes
Smoking them under midnight skies
Would put James Dean to shame
Glamorous in the pout of her lips
And scrappy when she'd try to pick a fight
She was the kind of treasure
That consumes you long before
You realize the inevitability of losing her
Girls like that don't stick around forever
Nor should they
It simply wouldn't be fair to other cities
To keep her here
She needed to run free
Finding new balconies at penthouses
To seduce beautiful strangers on
Skinny dipping in elegant pools
Life of the party that everyone
Seems to fall in love with
Though nobody really knows her
And truth be told, I don't think we'd want to

GOOD SAMARITAN

I don't like hearing
From other people
What you're up to
Or that you're living with her
A good Samaritan
Making honest money
For the first time
Having her thinking
You're something holy
And I won't tell otherwise
In my head
You're still depraved
Admitting to me
Your darkest secrets
As I scratched them away
Through a cloud of smoke
Forfeiting any reminisce
Of our dignity
In the woods behind
Someone's backyard party

A VOW OF INSINCERITY

Diamond earrings and cigars
On crimson leather chairs
Adorned with a trench coat
And a loosened pink tie
Into the night before satin sheets
Wrapped around us
In a silver dreamscape
Where we pray to the stars in the sky
That they coat us
For far-off tomorrows
Where we will dance endlessly
To the song of a promise
We know we'll never keep

CAT AND MOUSE

Pull me back
Into your world
This distance
Is killing me
Maybe even more
Than staying with you
Would have
Play with me
Cat and mouse
Trap me here
So that next time
I try to leave
I'll be
A little more wounded
And then I won't
Make it as far

GOD KNOWS I CAN TELL A TALE

I must be sick for missing you
My biggest fear, an evil in you
That I haven't seen in anybody since
The countless rumors that mortified me
And the sound of your cackle
As you'd brag about your conquests
Your lip turning up
And a smirk in your brown eyes
Taunting me, dangling promises
In front of my flushed face
I swore I hated you
That the sinfulness in your veins
Killed me inside
But God knows I can tell a tale
And truth be told
Your wicked touch
Was what made me come alive

COME ALIVE

I've been trying harder to remember you more vividly
My poetry is a homage to the longing I had for you
My music a liberation of a memory that doesn't haunt me
But it sure used to
You used to
Fear that once made ink-filled pages turn
And euphoria when I felt your hands on my neck
Hot breath in my ear
Causing my hair to stand on end
As my eyes challenged you to hold me harder
I miss the way that I'd try to quiet my breathing
As I'd sneak downstairs to meet you
Where you first made me feel alive
The fire in your eyes as you'd light up a joint
Suggesting we go back to your house
Equally terrified and thrilled
About what would come next

HAUNTING ME

I keep having delicious dreams
Where you're haunting me
They've gotten so vivid
That I take extra sleeping pills
With a few glasses of scotch
Just on the chance
I get you for half an hour longer
I'm disappointed each morning
By how easily I can
Wash you off in the shower

ADRENALINE

I was looking for trouble
For a shot of adrenaline
After long moments
Of unfortunate peace
I was restless
With a thirst for the unknown
The people I met along the way
Were searching for
The same kind of insanity
We were lost and
Pushed each other past
A point of self-discovery
And into a brilliantly chaotic
Sea of nightmares

BREAKING YOU

I tried to love you but I didn't know how
How to properly hold you
And try to trust you more than I could
To mean it when I smiled
As you talked about needing me forever
I stopped fucking you the way
That he taught me guys like you needed it
From girls who were willing to try anything once
To see eyes light up
Like you'd been taken to a heaven
You only pretended to believe in on Sundays
And I started making love instead
Gentle hips rocking
Dainty fingers tracing your face
Looking into your eager eyes
Slow and steady but somehow
I only ended up feeling dirtier
Like the softer I let you hold me
The more I was breaking you

I DON'T FEEL SAD, JUST OLDER

I've been feeling tired lately
Reminiscing about getting high and
Running down your street in the rain in LA
Glitter on our faces as she dances
For the world on a pole
Like it's the one thing
That's keeping her alive
As we laugh and chant
And Jackson has another bloody nose
We used to feel invincible
Like this small world wasn't ready
For how fast we lived
We used to feel this thrill
As we'd ride down the street
On the backs of motorcycles
Passing vacant beaches
Where we would stop occasionally
To get maybe an hour of sleep
I loved feeling on top of the world
With him on top of me
But now sitting in another club
I feel finished
Like I must have done and seen everything
So nothing excites me anymore
I don't feel sad, just older
Like when I was a little girl
I would go to the carnival
And dance and scream
As loud as I could
At the top of the Ferris wheel
We would egg each other on

To see who could brave the scariest ride
I would always win that competition
And by the time I stepped off the last one
I didn't want to stay any longer
Because I'd done the biggest thing
That I could do there
And there was nothing left to give me
That rush that I've spent too much
Of my young life chasing

FINE LINES

I've often found that with glamour comes tragedy
No amount of red lipstick and white powder
Could erase the mascara streaks that stained her face
When the lights turned from dim to black
The music faded and the blurry nights ghosted away
Into mornings too clear to kiss away the shame

SMELLS LIKE TEEN SPIRIT

We fell in love
To a Nirvana song
On a beautiful tapestry
Fishnets laced up her long legs
And I wore her lipstick
All over the bones of my hips
Fuck me
She whispered
I could have died right there
Tasting her heaven
Gave life to my thighs
And she filled me with a high
I still haven't come down from

COLLARBONE

My darling, you were maddening
And I loved you that way
I saw Ricky the other day
And it made me wonder
If she traces the scar on your collarbone
That you got the last night
We went to his house
When we drank a little too much
And decided to race our bikes
Down the hill behind his house
Before you hit that tree
And my white tank top
Started to soak up your blood
I wonder if she knows
The full truth about what happened
With the police later that night
As much as I love the idea
Of knowing that she's heard
Your lips say my name
The same lips you used to taste me with
At three in the morning
I think I'd rather you kept this from her
Maybe that would mean
That we still shared a secret
Nobody but us could understand

RED LEATHER

He wrote poetry with his lips
And crafted a home out of
Cigar smoke and red leather
Campfire secrets and
Starry eyed promises
Made under constellations
He taught me that I could
Love him and never understand him
Need him and run as far as I could
We were endlessly caught between
Something so beautifully magical
And something utterly devastating

MARCO POLO

You twirl your fingers through my hair
Your hands tracing my face
So lightly I question if it's real
A cigar between your lips
You whisper secrets in my ear
That dissipate into a cloud of smoke
And we play Marco Polo with our lips
Longing to make our way back to each other
You inhale my neck
And I gaze upward toward God
Relishing in every sin I commit
Under the comfortingly familiar
Weight of your body
As you rest between my hips
On the leather seats
In the back of your black Camaro

FAIRY DUST

Silver fairy dust coats your heavy eyelids
And your lashes flutter, tickling my cheek
Death bestows upon us
The most wondrous beckoning
For a taste of the freedom you give me
After long days of distantly watching the skyline
In prayer for a sign that we are indeed infinite
In the way that the fire ceases to burn
Singing campfire songs
For months of endless summer
And a promise more fatal, perhaps
Than knowing we won't kiss goodbye
Or have a last word

I WONDER IF YOU KEEP YOUR PROMISE

I thought about you tonight
For the first time in ages
I used to let my mind wander to you
Without restriction or hesitation
When we were a little younger
Until I grew tired because
I had replayed those nights together
Down to every perfect detail
And there was no mystery
For me to agonize over anymore
The crisp air as you opened the door
And the creak on the stairs
As you led me down to that couch
I can hear the scratched leather
From beneath your bare chest
My fingernails digging in
As my hips met yours for the first time
I was hooked on remembering
The widening of your brown eyes
As I learned how much
You really needed me
The first time you held me in a way

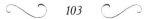

That I couldn't mistake for
Anything but what it was
We weren't the kids who grew up
Playing baseball in your backyard
Or laying on towels together at the beach
Telling secrets to the sand
You were a man that had been
Loved by many women
Myself the most fiercely
Until it wasn't enough for me anymore
And I find myself replaying
You in my mind tonight
A sense of eager restlessness
That has been missing from my life
Cursing myself for
Forgetting why I left you in the first place
And wondering if you still
Remember to hate me forever
Like you promised

RUNAWAY

That night was something out of his rock music
Metal scarring my face, blood on my hands
Wet to touch but free from any expected pain
Adrenaline in my veins, awakened
After a boring year of soft slumber
Helicopters above us and a desert so vast
With secrets that we could use to destroy them
But don't because we learned the hard way
That our voices meant nothing to the people
Who wanted to see us as monsters
And they didn't deserve the privilege
Of peeking inside the minds they deemed disturbed
Our fears were safer buried and guarded
Possibly for all of our eternities
If it meant not giving away parts of ourselves
That would be used to torture us without warning
Sirens weaving in and out of our ears
As we disappeared further away
From where they could find us
They still can't understand why we would leave
Risk everything that we'd ever earned
With a recklessness that damn near killed us
But we have no desire to lend our voices
To the people asking us things
That we should never have known how to answer

CHARLES

Little black dresses
Champagne in slender hands
Wrists wrapped in Tiffany
Trouble on your mind
Your wicked brown eyes
Teasing me
Across crowded rooms at parties
Your limo waiting downstairs
If you can sway me
Into believing I've been missing out
On a delicious ecstasy
That only you can give me
Stars dazzling my eyes
On the balcony of your penthouse
You clean off the razor
And cloak me in your coat
I used to feel infinite
Under your spell
A reckless bad boy
Turned businessman
Who was given everything
He ever wanted
Until you met a girl
Who wanted for nothing
But a thrill that no money or fancy toys
Could entertain

HISTORY BOOK

I love dreaming up
Forevers in my head
Jotting them down
And casting them
Into a history book
Of memories
Never carried out

HAPPY

I see you so happy with her
And I love seeing your smile
Wider than I've seen it in years
But it also kills me to realize
That I couldn't give you what she can
There's a lightness to her
That I've never had
An ease in the way that she holds you
I wanted so badly to hold you
And love you with all that I had
But something inside me
Stopped me from reaching out
And rubbing your back if you were down
From my eyes lighting up fully
When you'd kiss me and
Make promises that you meant
And it killed me to know
That there was a darkness inside of me
That you could never outlast

MY MIND HAUNTS ME

More than anybody else ever could
Nobody seems to understand
Why I laugh in the face of
The things that should terrify me
And didn't flinch the slightest bit
When he raised his fist at me
In front of a crowd of people
Partying to forget the loveless lives
They've sealed the fate of their futures to
If I'm being perfectly honest
And mind you there's no point
In lying to a notebook
That has seen tears and an inhuman wild in my eyes
I reckon those moments are
The ones in which I feel the most calm
Thoughts that were spiraling cease
For long enough for me to breathe
Reckless decisions put on pause
Because he was offering me a moment
Of sanity among the chaos of a mind like mine
Slowly becoming my salvation

BUTTONS

I miss the way that you would hold me
So tightly that I felt the buttons
On your collared shirt digging into
My warm skin from behind
Fears crumbling in your embrace
Forgetting about everybody else
The world was quiet and belonged to us
Dancing under navy constellations
And laughing as you'd kiss me
Standing in the middle of a thunderstorm
As we made promises they thought we didn't mean
But I know that we did
Even after life became a little too hard for us to keep them
And I began to think about you
Looking out of a window hundreds of miles away
I was never an easy girl to love
But you loved me anyways the best that you could
And I hope that you know
I'll be forever grateful to you
For understanding me more
Than I thought you could
Maybe I would be easier to love now
Though I'm afraid that's a question
That I'll never be able to bring myself to ask you

THAT ROOM

Old discolored white tiles
Two beige doors swinging loose on their hinges
The loud echo of footsteps following me
The wooden bench cold to touch
I hear the deep, metallic thud of the door locking
My body begins to stiffen
The chatter and laughter of other people fades away
Until I'm left with silence
Screaming loudly to me
Telling me I'm alone
It feels like a horror movie
Only this time there's no popcorn
I don't get to turn the lights on
I don't get to feel safe once again
Laughing at myself for being scared in the first place
As the credits scroll down the screen
Reminding me it's all pretend
Only this time it's not pretend
Never in my life have I felt so numb
Yet so aware of my body at the same time
Fear wells up inside of me
Stomach churning, palm sweating fear
The kind that instills the fight, flight or freeze response
That you learn about in psychology
I froze

HEAVY EYELIDS

Gleam in your eye like an
Angel seducing sin after sin
From my breath on your neck
The tide of your body
Crashing into mine
Wrapped in a bed of
Lilies and fever dreams
Of far-off tomorrows
In a precarious dive
Against sand that drains time
From heavy eyelids

OXYGEN

I didn't know what to do
When I lost you
Never mind that I could
Breathe
Without you
The laughter I had now but not by your side
Was no intensity
Compared to the pleas for belief
Each time I stood accused
Awaiting my fate
Our fate
Screaming matches and insecurities
The only things that could make us feel
Revenge a second nature
Getting high alone
Something to dry my eyes
The lows you would give me
Were something else
A disturbing way to show affection
But I would have chosen that every time
Over oxygen

ENDLESSLY

Black tar and black skies
Starry eyed and barely alive
An enigma, an angel
Deserving of all
And I'm falling
Apart without you darling
Greeting death like an old lover
Another way to disappear
I fear this time forever
I cared until I couldn't
I probably shouldn't admit
That I stopped thinking
That you could be saved
But it's people like me
Who willed you into the morgue and then to the grave
I still can't stop feeling this grief
The kind that cages me with no relief
Wars waging in my mind
As I long for the time
That I could hear you laughing
And saying my name

Because even in pain
You were selfless
You loved fearlessly, my dear
And it kills me when I hear
People call you selfish
For leaving when we left you
Long before you died
And now cry at night
Because we miss you
I miss you
Sitting here alone
Writing poems about your golden heart
And cartoon eyes
That I never took the time for
When you were alive
It's suffocating me, terrifying me
How final it is, as I'm saying goodbye
Guilt-ridden and good riddance
I shall miss you endlessly

I QUESTION MY RELIABILITY AS NARRATOR

As time grows further between
The person I was when I last held you
And the person I am as I reminisce
On what it was like to be loved by you
I question my own reliability as a narrator
Writing our story in the pages of worn notebooks
Sealing in ink a beginning and a middle
But no moment I can pinpoint as the end of us
Maybe that's because there wasn't a clear moment
Where you went from being mine
To being a stranger that knew all of my secrets
I wonder if you remember me
With the same passionate nostalgia
And if the moments I write about
Are the ones you think about
When you hear somebody say my name

HEAVY IN MY HEART

There are far too many things
That I want to tell you but
For now I'll keep them to myself
Maybe I will forever
Like how I never wanted to hurt you
And how seeing you nearly killed me
Because it wasn't me you were
On your way home to
I wanted to grab your hand
And ask you not to leave but instead
My eyes fell to the floor
And I made you think I hated you
Because it was easier
Than showing you how I was doing without you
How I wanted to tell you that I missed you
And ask you if I pop into your mind
Like you show up in mine
Uninvited but more magnetic than ever
How I lost something that I'll never get back
But will carry with me
Heavy in my heart until I die
How it ruins me every time
I think about the way that you found out
That I'd been hurt and hadn't come to you
How he took something from me
And I thought he destroyed me for good
Until you came along
And made me believe I was worthy
Of something better

DIRT CHEAP NOSTALGIA

What would it feel like
To see you after so long
And constant uninhibited vilifying
For the benefit of others
Would the wicked still sit
On your water lines
As you looked me up and down
Knowing you had all the control
And would prove me weak
And by charm or by force
Get exactly what you wanted

What would it feel like
To hear you after so long
Would the wear and tear
Of the dying young philosophy
You told me you adored
Take away that fire when you laugh
And your bony face creased
Finding those lines back
That had been missing for so long
Like forgotten smiles and pickup truck secrets

What would it feel like
To taste you after so long
Cinnamon and sativa like it did in the woods
Where my back was introduced to dirt
And I told you I was yours for the weekend
Before hanging up that leather
And putting on my cross necklace
Come Monday morning
Or would it taste cold and metallic
Like the blood I lost the last time
You sunk your lips into mind
And taught me I was a fool for trusting you

What would it feel like
To trace your body after so long
Would there be less of you since he died
And you turned to 80 proof and white lines
As a diet to make it through one more day
Would it feel distant
Because you'd know I was no longer a willing victim
To do with as you pleased
And would that make you feel like you lost something
That I would never admit
Belonged to you in the first place

WHISPERS IN RAINSTORMS

You were whispers in rainstorms
Fights in the middle of streets
About broken promises
And heaven between my hips
On a Saturday night

MY SILENCE

I fear that you must take my silence
To mean that I don't love you
The way that I once did
That I'm not thinking about you
Whispering the aching familiarity
Of your name between my lips
At two in the morning
When I should be sleeping
But am too busy dreaming
Your smile infiltrating my mind
With ideas that I can't
Just choose to forget
Your eyes keep me awake
You were the first person to really see me
Your arms don't hold me anymore
But your words wrap around me
Hot breath in my ear, pulling me close
As I take a few swigs to numb myself
From the memory of being loved
By the man that I can't bear to look at
When I know he isn't mine

JUVENILE ENVY

You were leather jackets and a hint of cinnamon
Diamond earrings and had three years on me
When you gripped my ponytail in the path
In the woods where you lit up the first blunt
I ever laid eyes on and you dared me
To take a hit, I assumed with my mouth
Little did I know you meant your fist
Just seven months later when all the girls were jealous
That I was with a real man
Their Danny Zuko bad boy fantasy
Played out vicariously through me
But they were too naive to know that you were my puppet master
Measuring every move I made
Ditching class and sneaking out each night
How was I still this far in and
Getting high on your tattooed chest
Where you wore the battle scar from your father like a hero
A slash across your collarbone
We were sewn together in the ugliest way
I had my own damage, which you never bothered to learn
As long as I bore every trauma on my body that you had to suffer
And kept drinking 40s under the bleachers with you and your
buddies
High-fiving them every time you told a sick joke
About getting lucky in the woods

RIDE OR DIE

I defined myself as your ride or die
Until you walked outside into the night
Emerald sky darkens on the streets we used to fight
But that didn't matter, I told myself
Until our wounds bled together in a puddle of hell
And I ached for you as I felt your pain
Didn't matter that my own heart was spilling down the drain
And my prints stained on the paper I used to write
Until it seeped so much that you couldn't see white
How is it that I still crave your touch?
The lovers that followed were never enough

NIGHTMARES

I've had dreams
Far sweeter than you
But none of them
As delicious
As the nightmares
You bring

MATCHSTICK

Loud music over the crackle of a matchstick
In the dim light of a hole in the wall bar
Where we make love to ghosts
And dance until we no longer crave
A desperate taste of dignity in a stranger's eyes
Bourbon laughter lining my lip
In another evening lost beneath tired constellations

JOYRIDING

I don't know exactly what drew me in first
Your fear of happiness
Your love of danger
Never meeting in the middle
And from that moment on neither did I
Jumping off that bridge plunging into icy water
Joyriding faster than lightning could strike
Thrill seeking at 3 a.m.
I walked finer lines than you snorted
Never feeling more alive
Than the euphoric moments
When I wasn't sure I would make it
Midnight shivers in snow
With your leather jacket
Draped around my naked shoulders
Looking into your wild eyes
Only visible from the flame of my matchstick

FEAR

What I fear more
Than your scream
Is the absence of it
For so long that
I forget the feeling
Of fear in my spine

DEMONS

Daydreaming of you
Writing about you and
Closing my eyes at night
With the hope of seeing you
After I sleep and just maybe
A glimpse of you in the dark
Grabbing my wrists
Cornering me in your bedroom
Will be enough to scratch
The itch I have for your darkness
My mind begging you
To be my biggest weakness once again
Longing to feel my lip tremble
The way it used to in your car
At 2 a.m. when I'd coat myself
In Daisy and dangerous fantasies
Of you not bringing me back
Safe and sound because
In the most twisted and beautiful way
I was in love with your demons
And you were in love with the way
That I'd dance for them

UNDER HEAVEN'S TAPESTRY

I think it would kill me
To find out that you don't
Romanticize faded leather
And the last hit of a cigarette
Being doused with rain
Under heaven's tapestry
The way that I do
Or the way that sunsets fade
Into nonexistent sleep
As dreamers cease to tire

THE LAST MAN TO TOUCH ME

The last man to touch me
Needed an infinite amount
More than I could give him
To look into his eyes and make promises
Rather than turning away
Because I couldn't look at him
While I was breaking him
And for me to relax
When he wrapped his arms
Too tightly around my body
Like if he gripped me hard enough
I would stick around a little longer
I can't bear to be with a man
Like that again
I don't trust myself
To stop being this selfish
Destroying him slowly
Because I didn't want to be alone

WITHOUT QUESTION

Wicked electricity
Causing your heart to beat
Beneath the ink on your chest
Taunting me because
I've never felt more alive
Than the night I realized
I feared you
And from then on
I loved you
Without question or reason

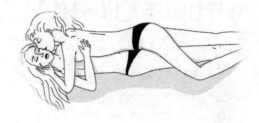

SAINT IN A PUSHUP BRA

We spilled secrets over bourbon
At the pub as we walked out
Under the midnight black sky
Your eyes undressing me under
The Little Dipper as I whispered
A lifetime of crimes and sins
We molded psalms
Out of the curves of each other's bodies
My head on your cleavage
Thinking maybe you could make me
Feel a little less hollow
Than I usually am
Worshipping your hands
Because they made me feel holy
And I fell onto my knees
Bruising them in prayer
And feeding fire to your thighs

BLACK CHERRY

Heart shaped sunglasses
My ruched top with cherries
Your hand on my shoulder
A fiery wild in your eyes
The first time I ever thought
About the temperature of leather
Was on my back in your BMW
A gateway to a heaven
That I never believed existed
'Sympathy for the Devil' on your stereo
As we drive by neon signs
Of my old stomping grounds
Where each shot was a rush
Of black cherry adrenaline
That feels minute now
Compared to each secret
Leaving your lips
So quietly that I question
If I'm making them up

RELAPSING

It's dizzying to fathom
Dazzling, even, how I got here
Addictive personality maybe
A desire to preserve a high
Long after the first signs
Of coming down because
I know the disgust
I will grace myself with
If I look in the mirror
I am all too familiar
With tossing and turning
For hours on end
Praying to a God that
I can't decide if I believe in
But I am willing to
If that's what it takes
To rid me of this ugliness
White powder shimmering
With temptation for a life
I thought was long behind me
A beautiful beginning
To a story with too many gruesome endings
Blood dripping down my face
A dryness in my head and eyes
In moments like these where
I question everything about myself
Selfishness snorted into self-hatred
Until finally I am back on the high
And I can't remember
Why I'm crying in the first place

MAYBE ONE DAY

Maybe one day
I'll write a poem
That isn't born out of
The way that you held me
And the hurt in my heart
When I lost you
But for now
I will indulge myself
Because I can't bare
The thought of
One day looking back
And realizing
That I've forgotten
What it was like
To be loved by you

FRIGID

I've found comfort in my fear
And I've run from the peace and calm
If you're used to losing your footing
It can make you feel balanced
In the midst of chaos
You stop waiting for things to go wrong
You know the ice will crack beneath you
And the frigid becomes your new normal

LAWLESS

She was lost with no friends
No family, no place to call home
I was lawless, liberated and tired of running
Damaged, exhausted
And needing something to keep ourselves sane
We were wrapped in each other
A hurricane around us
Dizzy from a lifetime of partying
Until we woke up one day feeling older
I was ready to sober up

Praying this time it would last long enough
For me to love her a little better
Than the last girl who fell for me

MOMENTARY THRILLS

I've spent too many nights
Sitting quietly under moonlight
Lonely and growing tired
Of swearing that I've paused my longing
For the momentary thrills
That I know won't cure me
And just may kill me
But are worth it to feel alive
In the most magnificent ways
That you're not supposed
To find beautiful

OCEAN EYES

Teeth scrape my ear
As your fingers trace promises
Across my collarbone
Your ocean eyes vibrant
And more pure than I've ever been
Lifetimes of discoveries
Dance around us
In a perfect tornado
I marvel as you melt
Between my thighs
And I lose
My train of

MY VISHNU

You fed off my darkness
Firecracker exhilaration
Taking you back many years
And in turn you gave me
A place to destroy myself
Slowly, one night at a time
Bearskin rug beneath our feet
Cabernet on my lips
Your tired eyes coming to life
We were drowning together
Addicted to our secret
We thought it was beautiful
Some dark fantasy
Lovers behind closed doors
Exchanging glances
Powerful enough to destroy worlds
And rebuild them all
You were tormented
By ghosts you couldn't talk about
And I never asked you to
My bones became fragile

In your embrace
I thought you needed me weak
We were damned
From the first time
I traced my fingers down your back
As I walked out of your office
And made you think
That I was capable of falling in love

SATAN LOVES ME WHEN I'M MANIC

Eyes wild, they make no contact
Smoke-filled breath on city streets
My mind racing faster than
Can make sense to anybody else
See, I'm always further ahead in my mind
Than I am in my words
Except for when I'm not
And the colors fade to gray
Stars above shrinking
And my attempts to connect a simple thought to an action
Become bleak
But that's not what you want to hear about is it?
The slow sand leaving my hourglass of life
Unable to drain quickly enough
You're here for the line of cocaine at midnight
That turns into the rest of someone's stash
Disappearing from glass tables
And the stranger that I give too much of myself to
Because it's 3 a.m. so bedtime is still a week away
And I need to feel worshipped
You want to hear about me laughing
While loud rock music plays

And I'm taking a shot or two or three
Until I've finished the entire damn bottle
Because in moments like these
I'm utterly hopeless at moderation
You like the eagerness in my voice
And relish in my reliving every bender
Filling in far more detail in my art
Than I actually remember
About a string of one-night stands
During a month or two or three
When being alone was particularly dangerous
And you know I used to be a good girl
But she faded away, nose out of a book
Eyes drifting back and forth
Between death and wildfire
Sick to my stomach, forever an entertainer
And just like you, Satan loves me when I'm manic

THAT WINTER

A crimson leatherbound notebook
Held all of our words that winter
If they read them, they'd be horrified
By the sins we committed so perfectly
Yet the ink on these tattered pages
Didn't convey a fraction of what we had
The power of our letters was limited
Compared to my hair wrapped around your fingers
And my flushed cheeks
When I saw you straighten your tie
From across the room and you caught me staring
For a little too long
I trace these pages, my eyes closed
And try to bring you to life
Wondering if you replay our last night
At your house like I do
Before I lost you for good

FINDING GOD

You can sleep with someone
And feel nothing but skin and bones
No less hollow
Than you feel when you're alone
And then God walks into your life
And the slightest brush of her hand
Against yours in the car
Can awaken every part of you

HIGH ON THE BOULEVARD

I was thinking about missing those
Gray skies that would loom overhead
Scaring away the tourists
I don't feel lonely anymore
And this sense of belonging is pure agony
Unusual girl, claiming my whole life
That I've been searching for a heaven
That keeps getting taken away
But I am a liar and God knows it
My hell is my vice
And I wasn't planning on
Getting clean any time soon
So call this state of static
A grave misfortune
My demons have shied away
I'm not fun to torment anymore
And I am craving the liberation
They would give me alone
With an empty bottle and my pen and paper
I was supposed to be a happy child
But pretending was tiring
And I started to feel
A little more dead each year
I wanted to feel alive

So I'd fall in love with strangers for a night
Thinking maybe I'd find a home in them
But I was out the door before morning
Praying in the backseat of a taxi
That this time I'd feel sad about it

WICKED WOMAN

She was a hot tempered
Insatiable maniac
The flame to my moth
For her I wanted to burn
To submit myself
To the first person who
Understood that I'd
Never been tamed
And was used to being
The one to bring the hell
I was infatuated
With being weak
For the first time in my life
Her egotistical tricks
Melted the blood in my veins
I fell in love with the
Wreckage she caused
Thanking God that I
Had the guts to fall
For such a wicked woman

FERRIS WHEEL

Can we try for a moment
To forget how damaged we are
Sitting back on that Ferris wheel
I want to think about
Wishing you would kiss me
And I want you to
Fall back in love with me
The way that you loved me
From beneath me
On that purple suede couch in your living room
Before I broke you
Past a point of feeling anything
Before you swallowed pills
To fill a black hole
That your parents created
I miss looking at constellations
Laughing about becoming
The cheesy type of couple
That used to make us gag
Maybe this is as good as it'll get from now on
Washing down sex with burning liquor
Drying our emptied eyes
Ghosts that don't know
What it's like anymore
To be loved

WHEN YOU LEAVE AN ARTIST

I dream of painting faces
That no longer resemble you
And falling asleep to anything
But the faint click of a menthol cigarette
When trains were just trains
Not tear stained letters
With heavy ink weighing me down
In a rumbling isolated car

SCENT OF REBELLION

Heathens whisper beautiful secrets
And I fall in love with the scent of rebellion
Spearmint on a Sunday night with
A pack of cigarettes and a stack
Of poker chips to come alive
Getting older, getting higher than we used to
Some kind of melancholic slow dance
Metal chains on our pants
Because we used to break curfew
But have no rules to follow anymore
And put our lives in the fate of
A fortune cookie, while making love
To the last match you can find
In your glove compartment

A THOUSAND MORE

Your clammy palms grazing mine
As you walk away
Ash falling to an earth that feels small
With the weight of your world
And mine colliding in time
With footprints on wet leaves
When you look back
My entire body squirms in anticipation
Because they don't understand
That for every promise you break
Your teeth on my bare shoulder
Are making a thousand more

YOU WERE MY HOME

I was robbed of you
My safety, my vice
The piece from
A past version of myself
That I still dream about
Longing for some type of closure
Whatever that means
My mind diluted
With too many memories
That include you
Beautiful and gut wrenching
When I was a little more broken
Than I am today
But God did I feel alive

BUTTERSCOTCH

Cherry red lollipops, purple fishnet stockings
Designer baby, sweeter than butterscotch
No one ever saw her parents, just a red Camaro
Driving too fast out of the parking lot
Started dreaming about men like him
Telling her she's special
He tastes like cinnamon
A hint of Marlboro Gold lingering
From a bad habit that he snuck on his lunch break
Thinking he can save her, doll face
Made up, dressed to the nines each morning
Hoping he'll look a little longer today
Family man, he's got something
That she'll never be a part of
But that's probably why he doesn't stop loving her
Damaged and lifeless, scars of youth
Burdening a girl too naive to know
That she's not infinitely desirable
She's an easy call to make in the evenings
No one looking for her, he needs the escape
Of a love like hers

Beyond her years in some ways
Temptation
She wants to lure him in, aging him back
Prom queen with a pill problem
And an attraction to men
That will inevitably leave her behind
If anyone comes around asking questions

MEANING

Lips tremble, hands unsteady
Grappling with mistaken identities
That we gave up for a dime
Because we learned a very long time ago
That we're all dying, some slower than others
Salt stained cheeks drying out
And the eyes of a man
That used to be a monster
Search my face
For some type of meaning
That I'll never be able to give him

INK ON PAPER

It is a luxurious naivety
To release yourself from captivity
Ink on paper reckoning for
A mountain of sins and secrets
And desires we'd forgotten about
With the trust that we will free ourselves
Because our notebooks
Will carry our burdens for us
Until another unusual soul
Reads our words and in a moment
Of inexplicable magic
Is saved a little bit from their haunting

A MAN I LOVED IN NEW YORK

Your tired hands graze the top
Of my dusty record player
Slow motion enchantment
Vintage daydreams
Beauty queens and chandeliers
Beckon to you on silver screens
Your longing growing more desperate
To dance with her one last time
Nostalgia becoming everything
Unable to live without looking back fondly
On a time that lifted you up under golden lights
At parties with parting stares
Of lovers that could have been
Shimmering dreams mere rosy ripples in champagne
Pastel skirts of every color
Spinning you into oblivion
Disconnecting you
From a world in front of you
You're painting your own place
To disappear to
A mind so full of youth for a time gone by
So enticing that I find my soul yearning for a past
That was history long before my existence

TEMPORARY

Grunge music and Rolling Stones tank tops
Mainstream beauty with an alternative mind
A little change in her pocket to buy a beer with
Or flip a coin to see which of us would die first
Conscience filled with mortality keeping her alive
Because everything she inhabited was temporary
And her existence felt threatened
By carrying out too long of a sentence on an earth
That never felt big enough to keep her as its own

WAITING FOR THE END OF THE WORLD

Charming and suave
Your rose lips blossom as we
Isolate ourselves
Overlooking a graying ocean with fog
So thick that my distant eyes
Try to make out your body
Shadowy Malibu figurines
Dancing together to
Different tunes the kids
Wouldn't recognize today
Echoing silence is our vow
Bonds as stretched as time
Without threatening to sever
For souls who take comfort
In desolate longing
Strange enough to be each other's
Silent company in a world
We wished to fade away from

SILVER SCREEN KIND OF WOMAN

Beautiful palaces and swans to serenade her
Making her almost entirely happy, just shy of content
A soul so lost for so long, reminiscing about days past
That they spent together, their minds electrified
With grand memories of laughing on sailboats
And dancing together in rose garden labyrinths
She felt so nearly perfect in his embrace after so long apart
But the years hadn't been kind enough to her
And nostalgia became easier for her than discovering
Herself in the gentle eyes she now found herself undeserving of

EMERALD SKIES OUT OF STORYBOOKS

They were filled with stars ensuing slumber
In young and restless souls lying beneath
Soft filters color her dreams
Magnificent Venetian alleyways
Where she can run free of captivity
Fantasies she had shied from yearning for
A glorious indulgence for a woman
Whose fate was sealed in slate
Many lifetimes ago

FLASHLIGHT TAG

I was burned out, my mind living far away
From my muddy Converse as we walked
Down streets we used to play flashlight tag on
Distant voices of our childhood
Playing eerily in my mind and I wonder
If you ever hear them too, if they haunt you
With suspended perfection just before
Everything went terribly wrong
When a handshake was just a handshake
And our lips held juvenile secrets from our parents
Before they were sealed shut from
Promises you could never unbreak
No matter how badly I know you want to

SURROGATE

I make love to strangers
Who are beautiful and mean
With unwavering distance
A surrogate for your love
That almost make me forget
You're probably doing the same thing
And I wonder if your ribcage
Tightens around your organs
As you gasp for air like I do
In the moments when
An unrecognizable face
Walks out the door again
And all I can feel is an urgent craving
To hear you laughing at me
Joint in your hand and
Bad decisions rolling off your tongue

PHOENIX

Leather tassels on my shorts
Smoke filled navy sky
Under stars that make us feel tiny
Desert loving looking like
Whiskey and rhinestones
Tipping the brim of your hat
In my drunken direction
Laughing about being too high
To worry about the things
That other people wrestle with
In their beds alone at night
Too stupid to know we were dying
Too momentarily blissful to care about
Just how broken we were

LET'S WALK INTO THE FIRE

Burn our bare feet as we escape
Rhinestone constellations
Aligning as we look up
At something much bigger than us
Cravings for a freedom
We won't find if we stay here
Leave with me, let's get out now
Discover something beautiful
And a little less broken
Than the best we could
Hope for here
Shed a single tear
A diamond for the memories
Burning heartaches
And fights that made us feel alive
For a passing moment in time
Then vow to never look back

WEAKER THAN I THOUGHT

I guess I'm weaker than I thought I was
Not speaking to you for the fear
Of looking into your eyes as I say hello
And not seeing them light up
The way they used to from above me
In the middle of the night
As you'd tell me you'd love me forever
Because I never thought
That you would go from being my world
To being my greatest muse
That I long for from afar
You carved a home for me
Out of gray sweatshirts
And hands that cradled my face
Like there was nothing more precious
In the world to you than keeping me safe
Your eyes held those stolen moments
As we would drive and watch movies
Your lips on mine and songs on car stereos
That were written for the two of us
It kills me that I don't know if you're as insatiable as me
Craving my touch and haunting yourself
With the way that your name sounded on my lips

WE WERE BURNING OUT YOUNG

Something about seventeen felt like
We were nearing an end
Of these golden ages
Smoking blunts on porches
Got us feeling a little bit
Closer to a heaven we decided
Not to believe in a long time ago
Seeing your eyes light up in the dark
Of our matchstick haven
Thinking we were standing
At the edge of the world

CON ARTIST

Con artist with a knack
For falling in love
In the in-between moments
When you craved a place
You could call home
Lies rolled of your tongue
Like they were made for me
And I'd never seen
Anything more beautiful
There was always a darkness
Inside of you
That few people knew existed
Earth shakingly volatile
A danger in the way you laughed
Like you probably wouldn't
Live to see another day

BETWEEN THE PAGES OF YOUR POETRY

You were dark, mysterious
A star waiting to be wished upon
Lusting after a girl
As damaged as you and she
Finally found a home
For the first time
Between the pages of your poetry
Where I found the perfect balance
Between peace and madness

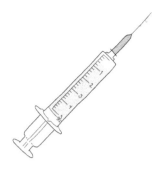

CHEAP PINK DRYWALL

I was lonely but insatiable
Neurotic and somehow desirable
To you when you were at your worst
Yet I still managed to carry you
Into the chilled water
And let you drown with me
Palm in clammy palm we were
Lost in each other so detrimentally
That the voids we tried to fill
Became bottomless pits
That no pills or sex
Up against cheap pink drywall
Could distract us from
Your baggage enchanted me
Because I knew I could give you
Something so sick and wrong
That would make you need me
Like a needle to your vein

MELANCHOLIC DUET

Oceans of greens and blues
Subdue our melancholic duet
Fine words, our scripture
Saddening even the sand
We crumble, softening
But never still in our embrace
The embers of a fire a few sunsets ago
Gave rise to a fury
You had toward me
Until aloofness
Silenced your cry for help
And I too fell victim to the protection
From our once lawless wild

CHAOTIC MIND

They were disappointed
That I couldn't be fixed
Insanity
Living alone inside my chaotic mind
That they could never understand
I've flown to manic heights
And I've woken up
On days they thought I wouldn't
Days I hoped I wouldn't
But I'd choose crazy any day
Over living inside a mind
That was numb for their comforts

MAPLE SYRUP

Dreaming about you
In bed, my stomach tightening
The lump in my throat
Threatening my oxygen supply
Thinking maybe I'll wake up tomorrow
To a phone call from you
Grief is in the air
As thick as the maple syrup
We put on our pancakes
After midnight
Cheering about the
Dollars we saved
In some Denny's parking lot
Hand in hand
Beneath Orion's Belt
As you told me you were more
Afraid of living than dying
And I'm angry at you
For getting what you wanted

PROMISES

Windswept kisses tease the sand
Laying on your towel
A hope like Gatsby dances in your eyes
We write promises on the beach
With the curls of our toes
That we keep until they are
Washed away by the tide
Holding me in your arms
Until the sun has set
And the heaven in your smile
Gets harder to make out
Under blackening skies

YELLOW JEEP

I miss being drunk under your eyes
Battle scars a point of pride
For a man who believes he's too far gone
For me to fall in love with
Trading war stories in the parking lot
My legs on your lap in the back of your dad's jeep
Outdoing each other with dares
Longing to be poisoned by you longer
As I prayed for the darkness of the night
To blanket us far longer than I knew it could

AN ANGEL

She was the prettiest mess I'd ever seen
Sadness a permanent feature in her eyes
Faking smiles to make the rest of us laugh
There's nothing like a beautiful girl with a golden heart
Drawing her last breath
To make your knees give in
And your palms press together in front of you
Bedside, asking a God you lost faith in a lifetime ago
To bring a moment of peace for everyone left behind
Who will never cease the grieving of an angel

GOODBYES

I can't keep lying to myself
Night after night
Sweet stories that you think of me
The way that I think of you
Lonely and longing
For something that was once so familiar
Aching to hold me
This time you won't be saying goodbye
I've said too many goodbyes
But yours will always be the most painful

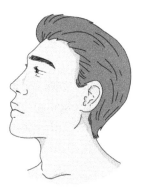

AFTER YOU'RE GONE

Your hand on the small of my back
Leather jacket on with your dark hair slicked
Dancing with me on the boardwalk under rain clouds
Ocean salt gracing your ink covered arms
Shrines for friends that you'd lost
And homage to a religion that you believed in for a moment
Perfume of whiskey neat on my neck
From the tease of your hungry lips
Writing poetry inside my head
For when I want to feel alive again
Long after you're gone

ROSE PETALS

I loved you like bloody feet
Walking on broken glass
That felt as soft as rose petals

CLEMENTINE SUNSETS

Picking flowers in vibrant grass
Pink saturation teasing me
Like *she loves me, she loves me not*
A poem for her here and there
I used to read her in the pages
Of every book from Salinger to Nabokov
Slow dancing in faded sundresses
Perfume on your neck like bonfire flames
And occasional flashbacks
Of stolen kisses on patios
When we were young enough
That we still had rules to break
And grown up enough to know
That clementine sunsets weren't infinite

BAD GIRLS DO IT BETTER

Tattoos on your arms
That scream loudly
That you like the bad girls
Street racing at 2 a.m. because
You learned at a young age
That money isn't everything
And your Porsche would
Make a magnificent coffin
Sick of your preppy life
Drinking wine coolers
In your parents' pool house
And calling that living
You need something dangerous
And the scotch
And devilish secrets
On my reckless lips
Are just the beginning

PASSION AND PERFUME

Navy blue skies above us
Your favorite song
Dangling between your lips
Carving out magic
Between pine trees
Cries for help at last silenced
Passion and perfume
Delight together
A sinful ambiance
And your hands were outstretched
Like your God had beckoned you
To claim the forest as your own
And present me as your offering

DARK PLACES

Cameras flashing, friends laughing
Strangers beneath me because
I learned a long time ago
That my mind is a dangerous place to be
Neurotic and obsessive
I can handle the hurt and the leaving
But I can't take the dark places
That my mind wanders to
If I come home too early
With not enough liquor in my veins
And I can't escape my demons
The ones that I loved until
My toxicity never crumbled away
Like it did for the other girls
Who grew up and decided
One day to love themselves
In a way I'll never understand

SUNSHINE IN BACKYARD PARADISE

Solitary summer state of mind
Thinking about train rides and jazz music
City getaways and falling in love
Reading faded pages of Fitzgerald
Laying on an aquamarine kaleidoscope
Vibrant tapestries beneath ripped denim
Cherry lips writing love songs
About afternoon tea and freckles
Wild in your heart, forever present
And dandelion seeds are filling my notebook

WINE INTO WISDOM

Diamond constellations
Making weary eyes dance
Tasting danger under moonlight
Wine into wisdom under cherry trees
And that wicked grin
Satin slip on a picnic blanket
Growing restless by the dread of sunlight
Your tired arms statuesque around my body

SACRED WHISPERS

Lemon trees hold tightly
Onto our silhouettes below
And we talk on the hill in the garden
Sacred whispers
About how one day we'll change
Laughing about a lost recklessness
That we aged out of
Unable to pinpoint when

AFTER EVERY BLAZING SUNSET

You talk about wanting to change for her
How you owe it to her broken memory
Static filling your mind
Haunting you with promises to a soul too lost
Asking for guiding clarity
That we both know she would laugh at
If she were still here
Before crushing a half-smoked cigarette into desert ground
And climbing into a car we don't recognize
Trying to kill herself a little bit more
After every blazing sunset
Until she finally did

LIFE NEVER CAME EASY

I was so sad and so free
For the longest time
Addicted to the wounds
That men would give me
Cursing the world
Because life never came easy to me
Until my emptiness
Was replaced by sadness
Being broken felt beautiful
After feeling nothing
For most of my childhood
And I relished every moment
That brought me to life
When another man
Would leave me
Or I'd drink too much at the bar
And cry in the bathroom
Until a pretty girl
Who was as broken as I was
Would ask me if I came there alone
Taking me back to her place
We would dance until her lips fused with mine
And the posters on her wall
Began spinning around me
Getting high and coming down
Feeling the world around me
Burning to ash
And thanking God
That red was my color

BURNT SIENNA SKIES

Oversized leather hats
We were trying to feel alive
In every way we could
Piercing someone's ear
In the back seat of a
Beat up Toyota Tundra
Laughing about her
Painting the sky for us
From heaven
Until our voices quieted
And we cried in silence
For the first time together
Since she died
None of us wanting to say
That we weren't all that far behind

7/11

I was completely enamored by you
Commanding and magnificently damned
You ruled your kingdom of the broken
All the way from Ricky's Garage
To the 7/11 by the mossed over graveyard
With terrifying protection
And promises to lost boys of a place to call home

STEREO

I drive in the car and listen
To your beautiful mind on stereo
I'll sell you a dream I had
Of us picking oranges
From trees in my garden
Static waves by the ocean
And all it'll cost you
Is refusal to forget me
Far off sequences of *I love you's*
And *I miss you's* and
I love you all over again

WALKS WITH THE BAD BOYS AND GIRLS

Owning the back alleys
Children were scared to run down
Popping bubblegum
Riding shotgun
In beat up convertibles
Flickers of lighters
Drinking boxed wine to save a dime
Costing us next to nothing
To live freer and far better
Than I had it uptown
Checkered blankets
And walks the woods
With the bad boys and girls
That lived across town
Moms and dads sheltering us
From the people more real
Than anyone we grew up knowing
I cursed that sheltering
I didn't know about living
Until I knew the smell
Of sprayed out gasoline
And the raised bumps of ink
On our arms from
Someone's mom's friend's sewing needle
Games of poker
Learning how to dull my grin
For a shiny penny
At an overcrowded kitchen table
The rumble of machines
From the attached laundromat
Knocking over pictures
Hanging on dusty rose wallpaper

And Kristy at the bathroom sink
Designing makeshift manhattans
In plastic champagne flutes
That didn't feel a beat out of pace

EYES OF THE WILD

My gratitude
Grows immeasurably
With the realization
That I am meaningless
In the eyes of the wild

MORE MAN THAN MONSTER

I think that in the end
You were more man than monster
Unshackled from the version of yourself
That you couldn't trust
Revenge that used to come so easily to you
Crumbling into brown eyes
That can't look up at me
And dandelion sunsets started feeling safe
You were kaleidoscopic madness
An untamable force to be reckoned with
And I your equally volatile counterpart
Now faded into a whisper in the wind
I think some days that we're just too damn quiet
Unharmed but unbewildered
Because we're too scared
That if we let ourselves live again
We'll live too much
And this time when you do something detrimental
We will have no sanctity to return to
We forfeited our safe haven, if you can call it that
Where forgiveness too often took the place of lingering resentment
And as I sit here next to you
Ghosts that touch fingertips lightly every now and then
Too much lost between us
I realize we've already said goodbye
Two lovers waiting until the end
No longer alive but not quite ready to die

AS A WOMAN

You were the first man to see me as a woman
To touch me as a woman, need me as a woman
No tremble in your hands when you cradled my face
Or apologies if you gripped my hips
Roughly enough to leave temporary fingernail indents
You kissed me like I was a woman
Who was used to being seen as a woman
Rather than some schoolgirl who found herself
Seeking out men like you to teach them
What it's like to be bent over the bed
And thought that making love was for fifteen-year-olds
Who found themselves momentarily in awe
Of a boy who walked them from the bus stop to their driveway
So we must have owed them something other than a simple thank you
You looked me up and down like a woman
Who was used to being the muse
Of many tired men
Brought to life by a girl who just discovered her womanhood
And after you finished, you held me
Like a woman who had been broken by a man for the first time
Discarded by a man like I went from
Everything to nothing within moments
And I hated you like a woman who spent her childhood hurting
And grew up with a hopeless wish
That being seen as a woman
Would change the way that she felt when she was called girl

SICK

I can't pinpoint the moment
That you went from being a monster
To being someone I'm sick enough to miss
Sick enough to write poetry for
The gate to my innermost vulnerability that I keep locked up
Only to visit on nights when I'm by myself with an empty bottle of wine
Sick enough to crave the touch that used to terrify me
During moments when I'm at my very worst
You know, there was a time when you were my very worst
Worst fear whose name I couldn't speak
Worst nightmare that kept me up for years to follow
Worst person I could have let back into my life
Because I was so damn certain
That there was something redeemable about you
And I needed someone to save
And that person sure as hell wasn't me

I'M NOT THAT GOOD

They thought I dated
Men like you because
I wanted to save them
But, honey, I'm not that good
You were the perfect place
For me to destroy myself
Where nobody would
Come looking

GOTHIC TIE-DYE

There is still that tiny sliver of me
That wants to stop being so nice
I want to be petty for a night, just one night
And show you all the fucked up entanglement in me
Like bedsheets and lies on a Sunday morning
I want to knock on the door
Of whatever hotel room you've trashed
And scream at you until my lungs deflate
Like tired balloons after everyone leaves a birthday party
Embarrass myself in front of the latest girl you made fall in love with you
And tell her that it won't last
Or maybe it will
Maybe she's easier than me, a maniac only in bed
A beauty queen who keeps her cool
Fucks you and stays unbothered
To hear you leave at 2 a.m. to drown yourself in vodka and pussy
But I doubt it'll last because you've never liked easy
You loved me insane, swapping ideas
Crazy trains bound to collide but closing our eyes
I want to spit on my dignity
If it means you'll see what has become of me since you left
I want to cry in your doorway
As you slam the white paint into my face
I want the girls crying in the club bathrooms
When the tequila hits hard the reminder that nobody is waiting up
for them
To have nothing on the mascara seeping into my face
Like gothic tie-dye on flesh

SELFISH

Why can't I just love you
The way that you need me to
You're sick of contingencies
And lies that everything is okay
I'm killing you night after night
With sex and then distance
And pretending that
I wasn't really pulling away
When you touched my arm
I've never been an easy woman to love
And you're not the first
That I'm no good for
But you're the first man
That I care about missing out on
When your eyes grow tired
Each day that you look at me
But I'm still too selfish
To let go of you

A MIND LIKE MINE

If your story sounds like this
Too much misery, too much bliss
A different person
When you flip the switch
Then I'm sorry
If you've got a mind like mine
I'm sure that you're drunk
All the time
Trying to kill your thoughts
Finding yourself at a loss
I'm at a loss
Because these highs they make me fly
Feel like a God, I'm in the sky
Invincible, I feel invincible
Until my brain gets overwhelmed
The pain is how I picture hell
It's a place that now I know quite well
Invisible, make me invisible

I know that I spend too much time
Locked inside this broken mind
Whether it's a safe place for me
I don't yet know
But at the end of the night
It's the place I call home
Getting high I'm in clubs filled with strangers
The danger doesn't scare me
As much as I scare myself
My health is suffering
Suffocated by the ecstasy

During the times when I'm feeling free
Manic in my company
The life of the party
These crowds, they love me

Their faces light up as they egg me on
It won't be long before I'm too far gone
But for now just enjoy it
I scream this order in silence
And try to forget what I know will come next
Making bets, with the cards in my hands
Turning heads
Hey, you want to have sex?

It's like I'm dreaming right now
Loud but I'm having a blast
I wish this would last
And I'm praying that this time
I won't come down too fast
I'll crash when I get there
The headaches will start
My heart feeling guilty
Feeling ashamed for feeling
So happy before
I'm so stupid to think that
I could have more

Now I'm hating myself
And I can't explain why
No one would understand
So why should I even try
Don't want to get out of bed
The idea of leaving the house

Shouldn't feel like too much
And I wish I was dead
Sometimes it lasts a day or two
Sometimes several weeks
I know a thing or two about feeling weak
Eyes leaking, it's hard to breathe
Don't want to talk to the person
Who's staring at me
Telling me not to worry
Because things will get better
But they don't ever get it
This illness in my mind
Changes faster than New England weather
And whether or not I know
That I'll be up again soon
Never seems to make a difference
It's the same old tune

You know I'd rather feel nothing
I'd rather be boring
Reassuring never works
For a mind like mine
But now I'm fine
I won't dwell on those lows
The show is just starting
In my house or at the park
Or at someone's friend's party
We drink and we laugh
I never turn down a dare
Let them stare, I don't care
They're just mere mortals down there
And now I'm finding myself
On top of the roof
I don't spook so easy

This, this right here
Is the rush that I crave
A grave with my name on it
Waiting if I make one misstep
But that's a bet that I'll take
If it gives me a break
From that crippling depression
Press on like you don't know
This high will soon be gone
They're chanting my name
Fame is all I want on nights like these
So, please I'm begging you
Distract me now with a story
Or something exciting
Let's race down the highway
Faster than lighting
I can't lose this momentum
Or I'll start to come down
Please don't let me drown

Out of the energy that I had before
I'm begging you, God
Just a half hour more
But once I start falling
There's no coming back
Until I've been through a lot
There has got to be a way
For me to feel better
Is there some sort of hack
To give me some sense of balance
Some sort of calm
But this war wages on
Caught between mania

And wanting to die
Would I feel some relief
If I just said goodbye

I know that's not an option
But a girl can dream
You know my mind is unusual
But they make it mainstream
Demons and angels
They love the contrast
They call it art
And they give us a contract
Because the fucked up
Seem to make the best type of art
Straight from the heart
To your iPods and your poetry books
If only you knew what it took
To be us for even a day
You see our successes but don't see us pray
For some sort of solution
To end this dismay

May I give you some food for thought
I'm not just a persona
I feel like this all the time
But you keep on subscribing
Because I make my pain rhyme

CPSIA information can be obtained
at www.ICGtesting.com
Printed in the USA
BVHW082248170521
607554BV00007B/1386

9 781737 091547